in
the
news™

HOMELESSNESS
IN AMERICA TODAY

Jennifer Bringle

ROSEN
PUBLISHING®

New York

Published in 2011 by The Rosen Publishing Group, Inc.
29 East 21st Street, New York, NY 10010

Library of Congress Cataloging-in-Publication Data

Bringle, Jennifer.
Homelessness in America today / Jennifer Bringle. — 1st ed.
   p. cm. — (In the news)
Includes bibliographical references and index.
ISBN 978-1-4358-9451-8 (library binding) —
ISBN 978-1-4488-1683-5 (pbk.) —
ISBN 978-1-4488-1691-0 (6-pack)
1. Homelessness—United States—Juvenile literature.
2. Homeless persons—United States—Juvenile literature. I. Title.
HV4505.B69 2011
362.5'20973—dc22

                                                 2009052450

Manufactured in the United States of America

CPSIA Compliance Information: Batch #S10YA: For further information, contact Rosen Publishing, New York, New York, at 1-800-237-9932.

On the cover: Top left: Because of rising joblessness during the recession, foreclosures have increased in the United States, forcing more people into homelessness. Top right: Often trying to escape a troubled home life, many young runaways in the United States end up living on the streets. Bottom: Many people who've lost their homes due to foreclosure have been forced to live in tent cities, like this one near Sacramento, California.

contents

Homelessness: An Overview

When you say the word "homelessness," most people immediately think of people living on the street or sleeping in city parks. But the reality of homelessness is far more complex, especially in the wake of a struggling economy.

A person is considered homeless if he or she lacks a fixed, regular, and adequate nighttime residence. People are also considered homeless if they regularly spend nights in homeless shelters and other such facilities. Therefore, while people who sleep in parks fit the definition of homelessness, so do families that rely on relatives for temporary shelter, or individuals who sleep temporarily in shelters or even vehicles. A homeless person could be a classmate whose family finds shelter in motels, or the woman sitting next to you on the bus who stays with friends after having lost her house.

Because of this, determining the exact number of homeless people in the United States is difficult. For most of those who don't have a permanent home, the condition

Joblessness has hit America hard during the recession. As a result, many have lost their homes, and some homeless people are forced to live on the street.

is temporary. But according to a study by the National Law Center on Homelessness and Poverty, approximately 3.5 million people—1.35 million of them children—are likely to experience homelessness in a given year. Those numbers surfaced around the beginning of the nation's economic crisis in 2007. This crisis increased the number of people who don't have a permanent residence. Many people found themselves unemployed and unable to pay mortgages or rent, and they were forced out onto the streets or into the homes of friends or family.

What Causes Homelessness?

Due to the recession's high foreclosure rates, many people in the United States have lost their homes.

The Center on Budget and Policy Priorities says reaching a national unemployment rate of 9 percent or higher could cause the number of poor Americans to rise by 7.5, to 10.3 million. And the number of deeply poor people—those with incomes below half of the poverty line— could rise by an estimated 4.5, to 6.3 million. That would, in turn, result in 900,000 to 1.1 million families with children falling into deep poverty. Being in that financial state puts people at risk of housing instability and homelessness.

A growing housing market crisis only makes the problem worse. Foreclosure, which is a lender's legal termination of a homeowner's loan (usually after the homeowner can no longer make payments), has forced many people to give up their homes. Because of this, many families must turn to rental properties for housing. This drives up rents and reduces availability, making rental housing less affordable. Since poor people generally rent, many of them find themselves unable to find affordable rental housing as well.

The troubled economy is just one of the causes of homelessness. People find themselves without a permanent residence for a number of reasons, including:

- Poverty. One of the top causes of homelessness is poverty. Two factors contribute to growing poverty levels in the United States: decreasing employment opportunities, and the lower quality and availability of public assistance. And with the recession putting more and more people out of work, public assistance systems are stretched even more thinly than before. This leaves too many people needing help—and not enough help to cover their needs.
- Lack of affordable housing. A growing population of poor people, coupled with a decrease in the availability of affordable housing, means that many more people will find themselves homeless. The more people who lose their homes and are forced to move into rental housing, the less rental housing there is for even poorer people. In addition, the limited scale of housing assistance programs means that fewer impoverished people can receive help paying their living expenses.

- Domestic violence. Battered women who live in poverty must often choose between staying in an abusive relationship or becoming homeless. According to the National Coalition for the Homeless, approximately half of all women and children experiencing homelessness are fleeing domestic violence. Many times, battered women don't have jobs or don't make enough at their jobs to support themselves and their children. In these situations, they often cannot rely on any financial support from their spouse or significant other, as that person is usually the one they are fleeing.

- Mental illness. Since many impoverished mentally ill people cannot afford the proper treatment or supportive housing they need, they find themselves on the streets. According to the U.S. Conference of Mayors, approximately 16 percent of the single adult homeless population suffers from some form of severe and persistent mental illness.

- Addiction. Drug and alcohol abuse, especially among those already suffering from poverty, often leads to homelessness. Many of those who are addicted to drugs and alcohol find it hard to stay employed. They fall so deeply into their addiction that they can no longer afford to pay for housing or otherwise support themselves.

They cannot afford the counseling or support that is needed to combat addiction. The connection between addiction and homelessness is complex, though, as not all addicts end up homeless. In this scenario, the presence of poverty definitely increases the likelihood of an addict becoming homeless.

Who Are the Homeless?

With an increase in the homeless population, people who would have never imagined being homeless find themselves in that exact situation. The growing shortage of affordable housing and the huge increase in poverty and joblessness mean that families and children end up living without a home. This phenomenon—made worse by the recession and the housing crisis—has changed the makeup of the homeless population in the United States.

There are several groups that seem hardest hit by homelessness. One of the major, and least recognized, groups is children. According to the National Coalition for the Homeless, children under the age of eighteen account for more than a third of the homeless population. Nearly half of these children are under the age of five. According to the National Law Center on Homelessness and Poverty, around a quarter of the homeless population are between the ages of twenty-five and thirty-four, and less than 10

Because of job loss and poverty, some families can't afford permanent housing. Often, they find themselves living with family, in shelters, or, in the worst cases, on the street.

percent are fifty-five to thirty-four. While it may seem unbelievable, many homeless people are children and teens.

As far as gender goes, the single homeless population is most likely to be male. But single men only make up some of that population, as families account for a large portion of the homeless population in the United States. In many of the major urban areas, families and single mothers with children make up around a third of the homeless population. In rural areas, those numbers are thought to be even higher.

When it comes to ethnicity, African Americans make up a majority of the homeless population. According to the U.S. Conference of Mayors, African Americans account for nearly half of the homeless populations of major U.S. cities. Caucasians come in a close second, representing more than a third of the population. Hispanics, Native Americans, and Asians follow behind as much smaller percentages.

Other groups that tend to be largely represented among homeless populations are victims of domestic violence, veterans, persons with mental illness, and those suffering from drug or alcohol addiction.

Numbers and categories on paper might not be that meaningful to those reading about homelessness in a book. However, this information does show that homeless people are often just like everyone else. They don't always fall into an easily recognizable stereotype or profile. They are simply people who, for one reason or another, find themselves without a place to call home.

The Recession's Effect on Homelessness

I t is hard to turn on the television or pick up a newspaper without seeing something about the economy. In the past few years, bank failures, rising foreclosure rates, and job losses have put our country's financial position into crisis. The situation has gotten so bad that we have slipped into a recession. While people often use the word "recession" to describe what's happening, what does it really mean?

A recession is a general slowdown of economic activity for a prolonged period of time. This slowdown is measured in several different ways, such as:

- Low employment numbers. When employment numbers decrease and more people go jobless, it negatively affects the economy.
- Low investment spending. During economic downturns, many people cannot afford to invest money in things such as stocks and bonds. They also cannot afford to invest in property or homes.

- Low household incomes. A large drop in the average household income is often a good indicator of a struggling economy. When people make less, they spend less, and that slows the economy.
- Low business profits. When the economy struggles, many people don't have money to spend. That, in turn, causes business profits to decrease.
- Low gross domestic product. Gross domestic product (GDP) is a basic measure of a country's economic performance based on the market value of goods produced within that country. In other words, a country's GDP is a measurement of the value of its export products, such as food, cars, or other items.

When people lose their jobs, they often file for unemployment benefits. The recession has caused record numbers of people to file for unemployment.

When people talk about the recession and the state of the economy, they often mention the word "depression" as well. A depression is far more serious than a recession. It is defined by a decline in the GDP of more

During the Great Depression, many people were out of work and could no longer afford food. Many of them stood in long breadlines for food from charities.

than 10 percent, or a decline that lasts more than three years. The last depression was the Great Depression of the 1930s. After the Great Depression, many laws and government agencies were put into place to prevent such a severe economic crash from happening again.

A recession can affect any family, even those with a steady income. Many companies that struggle during an economic downturn cut or reduce employee benefits, such as retirement plans, bonuses, and even health insurance. Often, these companies also freeze raises, meaning that employees don't get the regular pay increases they depend on. Some companies may force their workers to go on furlough, or take unpaid days off, to help save the companies money. When these kinds of things happen to workers, they may suffer a financial burden and even be unable to pay bills or afford what they once could.

In more extreme cases, the recession causes businesses to close altogether or lay off workers that they can no longer afford to pay. When people get laid off, it means that they are let go from their jobs. It's different from being fired because it is not based on any wrongdoing on the employee's part. Often, laid-off employees will get some sort of severance pay, which is usually a portion of their regular salary and is based on how long they worked with the company. Workers who have been laid off may also qualify for unemployment benefits, which is money a person can receive from the government for a limited period of time after losing his or her job. Unemployment benefits are usually less than the salary a worker would have made at his or her job, but it is a way to still have a little income while looking for a new job.

With so many people losing their jobs, finding a new job can be difficult for the unemployed because too many people are competing for the same positions. That means if a parent loses his or her job, he or she can go a long time without finding a new one. With no job, the parent won't have the income to pay bills, mortgages, or rent, or buy things that his or her family needs.

Homelessness by the Numbers

Whenever people talk about homelessness and the recession, a lot of statistics get thrown around. While it is important to measure the impact of the recession and homelessness, what do all of these numbers really mean? What follows is a breakdown of the statistics that are more commonly used in reference to the recession and the homeless.

Unemployment Rates

Each month, the Bureau of Labor Statistics of the U.S. Department of Labor announces the unemployment numbers. Those statistics are based on a monthly sample survey done in about sixty thousand households across the country. While that may not sound like a lot of people, as far as survey samples go, it is actually quite large. This gives a general estimate of the number of people who have lost their jobs.

Foreclosure Rates

Foreclosure rates are calculated by the number of foreclosure notices, default notices, auction sale notices, and bank repossessions that are filed each month. These numbers are compiled and published by companies such as RealtyTrac. The important thing to remember about foreclosure rates is that for each foreclosure, there is a family without a home.

Bankruptcy Rates

Filing for bankruptcy means making a legal declaration that you cannot pay off your debts. People who file for bankruptcy are no longer responsible for all or most of

Job losses have left many Americans struggling to pay their bills. Because they don't have a steady income to cover their expenses, some are forced to declare bankruptcy.

their debts. But as a result, they receive bad credit scores and suffer other negative financial consequences. Filing for bankruptcy is a last resort when a person gets so far into debt that there is really no other way out. When people file for bankruptcy, those numbers are reported to the Administrative Office of the U.S. Courts, which compiles statistics on bankruptcy filings for each quarter in December, March, June, and September.

Homelessness Rates

Homelessness rates are difficult to measure because the homeless population changes so often. Another difficulty is conflicting methods of calculation. One method involves researchers attempting to count all of the people who are literally homeless on a given day or during a given week. This method is called a point-in-time count, and it can cause researchers to overestimate the numbers. Another method, called period prevalence, examines the number of people who are homeless over a given period of time. This method can also give misleading numbers because homeless populations differ during different times of the year. The U.S. Department of Housing and Urban Development (HUD) has issued standardized reporting requirements that include both those inside the system (in shelters) and those outside of it (not living in shelters) using a point-in-time count.

A lot of talk about the recession is put in the context of numbers. Whether it is unemployment rates, foreclosure rates, housing costs, or GDP percentages, numbers seem to tell the story of how the recession is affecting the United States. But the important thing to remember is that behind those numbers are millions of people who make up those statistics. They are people without the jobs, without the homes, and without the money to care for themselves and their families.

Homelessness and Kids

Many people think that all homeless people are adults. But in truth, the homeless population in the United States is comprised of a lot of children and families. Kids whose families can no longer afford permanent housing may find themselves living in shelters or hotels, with relatives, or, in extreme cases, on the streets.

According to the National Law Center on Homelessness and Poverty, more than twenty-five percent of the homeless in this country are under the age of eighteen. Over the past decade, the number of homeless families with children has increased significantly. In fact, this type of family is among the fastest-growing segments of the homeless population, especially in the wake of the recession. According to the National Center on Family Homelessness, one in fifty children in the United States experiences homelessness each year.

In schools across the country, children who don't seem any different from their classmates deal with the

Though many people think of homeless people as older men, a large number of the homeless in America are children and families.

stress of not having a permanent home. According to the National Association for the Education of Homeless Children and Youth, the number of homeless children enrolled in public schools has significantly increased. During the 2006–2007 and 2007–2008 school years, there was a 17 percent increase in the number of homeless students. Even more troubling, homelessness is often underreported in this situation, so there may be even more schoolchildren without homes.

So how do these children become homeless? A number of factors can contribute to child or family homelessness, such as:

- Poverty. When parents don't earn an adequate wage or lose their jobs, they can no longer provide for their family. This puts both the parents and their children at great risk for homelessness.
- Lack of affordable housing. Because housing prices have risen, many people with low-income jobs cannot afford even rental housing. According to the National Center on Family Homelessness, a full-time worker earning minimum wage cannot afford a one-bedroom apartment priced at the fair market rent anywhere in the United States. Therefore single parents, or even two-parent families working low-wage jobs, may be unable to afford housing. And if one of those parents loses his or her job, there is an even higher risk of homelessness.
- Domestic violence. Parents and children fleeing domestic violence situations often struggle to find permanent housing. Limited income and limited ability to enforce child support make it hard for those leaving violent relationships to provide for their children.

Because of trouble at home, some kids run away to escape. But once they leave, many of them are forced to live on the street or in shelters.

- Running away. Among the young homeless population, there is a small percentage of unaccompanied minors. These children and teens have often been thrown out or abandoned by their parents, or they have run away from home. Reasons leading up to this can include abuse, neglect, substance abuse, or extreme family conflict.

Homeless Life

When parents lose their jobs and can no longer afford to pay the mortgage or rent, their children suffer right along with them. They often don't have access to the same conveniences that their non-homeless peers enjoy. It goes beyond just not having new toys or being able to afford the latest video game. Homeless children sometimes have to go without food, warm clothing, health care, and even shelter. This can negatively affect a child's life in a number of ways, both physically and mentally.

Homeless children are often at much higher risk for disease and sickness. In fact, homeless children get sick four times more often than other children. They experience four times as many respiratory infections and twice as many ear infections as children with permanent homes. They also have four times more gastrointestinal (digestive system) problems, and they are four times more likely to have asthma than other kids. Homeless children often don't have access to affordable health care, so their illnesses go untreated or undiagnosed.

In addition, homeless children go hungry at twice the rate of other children. Although it may seem like a contradiction, homeless kids also experience a higher rate of obesity due to nutritional deficiencies. Many healthy foods, such as fruits and vegetables, can be

Homeless families often depend on shelters for food and a place to sleep. Shelters across the country have seen an increase in patrons as the economy worsens.

more expensive than less healthy choices. And if a family doesn't have a home, they don't have a place to cook meals. That means they rely on prepackaged food and fast food, which is often high in fat, cholesterol, and sodium, and low in the vitamins and minerals that children need to be healthy.

As if those physical problems weren't bad enough, children without homes have three times the rate of emotional and behavioral problems than children with permanent homes. The additional stress of not knowing where they'll sleep, or sharing cramped quarters with several family members, can wear on children. Not having new or clean clothing, or access to facilities for regular bathing, can cause a child to be teased or cast out at school. This can affect the child's mental and emotional well-being.

If a homeless child suffers from a learning disability or other mental condition, such as attention deficit disorder (ADD), dyslexia, or anxiety, he or she often goes undiagnosed. Even if these children are diagnosed, their parents usually cannot afford the medicines or treatment for the condition. They also face the challenge of advocating on behalf of their children while facing the stresses of their own homelessness or joblessness.

The physical and emotional problems that homeless children can face are bad. But there are many other negative effects of homelessness.

Violence

Many homeless children are the victims of violence. According to the National Center on Family Homelessness, 83 percent of homeless children have experienced at least one serious violent incident by the age of twelve. And almost a quarter of all homeless children have witnessed acts of violence within their own families. Children who experience violence are more likely to exhibit frequent aggressive and antisocial

Homeless children often struggle in school more than their counterparts with homes. They worry about not having enough food or a safe place to sleep, making it hard to focus on schoolwork.

behavior. They also often have higher levels of fearfulness, depression, and anxiety. In addition, homeless children tend to accept violence as an acceptable means of resolving conflicts.

Developmental and Academic Challenges

According to the National Center on Family Homelessness, homeless children are four times more likely to show delayed development. And they are twice as likely to have learning disabilities than those with permanent homes. Because many homeless children move a lot, they change schools more often and thus have a harder time establishing a reliable school routine. This may result in difficulty establishing stable peer and teacher relationships. These children may also lose high school credits when transferring to new schools.

Homeless children lead highly stressful and uncertain lives. They often don't know where they'll sleep at night, or whether or not they'll have healthy meals. Just like other kids, it hurts them to see their parents unhappy. And unfortunately, homeless parents struggle tremendously and are often sad and suffering from stress or anxiety. For a variety of reasons, the life of a homeless child is a very difficult one indeed.

Homelessness Across the Country

American cities are struggling under the burden of the housing crisis during the recession. Unemployment and foreclosure rates are rising, and many cities are having a hard time accommodating the increasing number of people who are losing their homes. That means a lot of cities have a large number of homeless people living in shelters, temporary housing, and even on the streets.

Nearly two-thirds of the nation's homeless population are centralized in urban areas. Less than a third are located in suburbs, while less than 10 percent reside in rural areas. Homeless populations for cities and states are calculated in two different ways: by the actual number of homeless people and by the rate, which is calculated by the number of homeless people in relation to the population of the city/state.

According to the National Alliance to End Homelessness, one of the top cities for homelessness in the United States is Los Angeles, California. That's no

It's pretty common to find homeless people sleeping on the street in many cities. Due to the recession, the homeless population has increased, overcrowding many shelters.

surprise because the state of California is one of the hardest hit by the recession. It is deeply in debt, and foreclosure rates have skyrocketed. Those factors, along with staggering unemployment, mean that many individuals, as well as families, are finding themselves without permanent homes. The city's mild climate also makes it a prime place for homeless people to live. Because the weather usually doesn't get extremely cold, it's easier for the homeless to survive on the streets.

Another area experiencing high rates of homelessness is Detroit, Michigan. Once the prosperous home of

The decline of the auto industry has hit Detroit, Michigan, hard, causing a major increase in homelessness. Some without homes in the city are forced to create shelter from scraps they find on the street.

the American auto industry, Detroit has struggled right along with the automobile manufacturers. As the economy dropped, people could no longer afford to buy new cars. Even when they could, the "Big Three" car companies—Ford, General Motors, and Chrysler—had trouble keeping up with foreign competitors.

Many people who worked in the auto plants have been laid off. Those who worked in other auto-related fields, such as parts manufacturers, car dealers, and mechanics, have lost their jobs, too. Because so many people in Detroit and other parts of Michigan have lost their jobs, there are many people losing their homes. Thus, there are a lot more homeless people.

Another part of the country that has been hit hard by homelessness is New York City. New York has long had a problem with homelessness. But with the recession, the city's homeless population has grown significantly. With New York's struggling banking and publishing industries, a lot of professionals have lost their jobs. Many of these people have turned to lower-paying and temporary jobs— jobs that low-income workers once relied on. And because housing in the city is limited, rent and mortgages are much higher there than elsewhere in the country. Together, all of these factors mean that many people can't afford housing and must turn to friends and family, shelters, and sometimes the streets for a place to sleep.

Warmer states, such as Georgia and Florida, have also seen significant increases in their homeless populations. While these areas have more homeless people due to the same economic problems that cities like Los Angeles, Detroit, and New York have, there is another big reason why their homeless populations have grown: the weather. Warmer climates are much more appealing to those who live on the streets. In northern cities, winters are harsh and often deadly. For those living on the street, freezing to death is a real fear during cold winter nights. But in warmer southern states, winters aren't as

Due to shelter overcrowding, and a lack of affordable housing, homeless tent cities have popped up in many cities, such as Sacramento, California.

harsh, so life on the street is more tolerable.

Effects of Homelessness on Cities

The rise in homelessness due to the recession has had a major impact on cities. With more people living on the streets or in temporary housing or shelters, an even greater strain is put on the social services and law enforcement divisions of cities. Since many city and state budgets are already stretched because of the economic downturn, the growing homeless population just makes a bad situation even worse.

One of the main effects of the rise in homelessness is the demand for shelter. In many cities, there are not enough shelters to meet the demands of the growing number of people without homes. Some cities have tried to build new shelters or convert existing buildings into shelters, but such projects cost quite a bit of money. And during this economic crisis, extra money is something that many cities just don't have.

Because of the shortage of available shelter, many homeless people find themselves living on the street. In many urban areas, such as Fresno, California; Seattle, Washington; and Sacramento, California, tent cities have popped up. In these encampments, homeless people gather and build tent shelters reminiscent of the shanty-towns erected by the homeless during the Great Depression.

Homeless camps such as these—as well as home-less persons living without shelter on the streets—pose another major problem for cities. When large numbers of people live on the street, there is usually a need for additional law enforcement to deal with crimes commit-ted by and against homeless people.

It may seem that people living on the street are trou-blemakers or are more likely to commit crimes, but that is often not the case. Most crimes committed by the homeless are petty in nature and include offenses like public intoxication, open-container violations, loitering, and trespassing. Crimes committed against homeless people, such as robbery, assault, and even murder, are far more common than violent crimes committed by the homeless.

Regardless of who is committing the crime, police officers and medical emergency crews must respond to the situation. This costs the city money, as well as the time and attention that those responders could devote to other crimes or emergencies.

A larger number of homeless people means that there is a greater need for food assistance. According to a survey by the City Mayors Society, many cities hardest hit by the financial crisis have experienced an increase in demand for emergency food assistance. This report also found that the number of people requesting emergency food assistance for the first time has increased.

An increased demand for food, along with higher food prices, results in a strain on city resources, as well as a shortage of food for those in need. Many cities' food pantries and soup kitchens have been forced to purchase less food due to high prices. Because they have less food and a higher demand, some have had to turn people away or reduce the amount of food that they give.

Another problem associated with the growing rate of homelessness is the ability to provide health care for the homeless. The homeless and those living in extreme poverty often suffer from serious health problems such as tuberculosis, AIDS, malnutrition, and severe dental problems. Conditions that also occur in people at higher income levels—alcoholism, mental illness, diabetes, hypertension, and physical disabilities—are especially prevalent, and often go untreated, in the homeless population. Undetected and untreated communicable

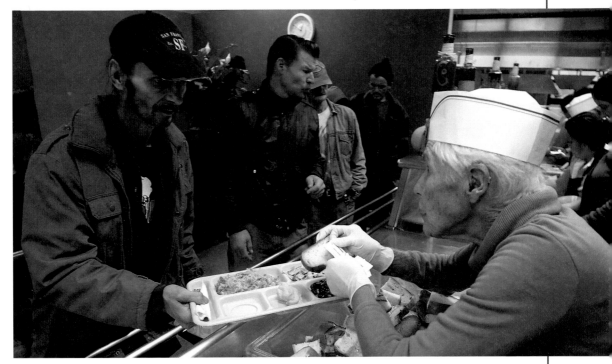

When people can't afford housing, they usually can't afford other necessities, such as food. Soup kitchens work to feed the nation's growing homeless population.

diseases can easily spread through homeless populations and even reach the general public.

Most homeless people do not have health insurance, nor do they have the cash to pay for medical expenses. They often do not live near health care facilities, and they usually have no means of transportation other than walking. Because of these factors, and the fact that many homeless people are more concerned with meeting immediate needs like shelter and food, many let health problems go until they become major issues. Once a minor health problem turns into a medical emergency, many people without homes or access to regular health care are forced to go to a hospital emergency room or an urgent care clinic for treatment. When this happens, the cost of treating these people rests on government and taxpayer money.

The growing population of homeless people in cities presents a complex problem. As the recession continues, the population of those unable to afford a permanent home is bound to increase. Though many cities struggle during difficult economic times, they still must find solutions to deal with this major problem.

How They Are Coping

Cities deal with their homeless populations in a number of ways. In some places, the homeless are criminalized and arrested for such crimes as trespassing and panhandling (asking for money or other handouts on the street). Other cities have looked for alternative methods of dealing with the problem of homelessness.

The National Law Center on Homelessness and Poverty and the National Coalition for the Homeless released a report, "Homes Not Handcuffs," on the criminalization of homelessness. The report details some of the laws cities have passed that target the homeless, and it ranks the top-ten cities in the United States with the worst practices in regard to criminalizing homelessness. These cities are dubbed the nation's top-ten "Meanest Cities."

The "Meanest Cities" list is based on various factors: the number of antihomeless laws in the city, the enforcement of those laws, the general political climate toward homeless people, and the city's history of criminalization measures. Laws that target the homeless include those that make it illegal to sleep, eat, or sit in public spaces, and those that punish people for begging or panhandling. The report lists Los Angeles, California; St. Petersburg, Florida; Orlando, Florida; Atlanta, Georgia; Gainesville, Florida; Kalamazoo, Michigan; San Francisco, California; Honolulu, Hawaii; Bradenton, Florida; and Berkeley, California. One example of the reasoning behind this ranking is a study conducted by the University of California, Los Angeles (UCLA). The UCLA study found that the city of Los Angeles spent more money on law enforcement intended to crack down on homeless crimes like loitering and jaywalking than it did on trying to solve the problem of homelessness to prevent the crimes from happening in the first place.

While these reports and lists reflect a growing problem, they don't tell the whole story. Many cities have experienced such large increases in homelessness in such a short amount of time that they just don't know

Many homeless people are arrested each year for panhandling on city streets. Some advocacy groups think this isn't an effective way to deal with the problem.

how to handle the problem effectively. And many of these cities' governments are struggling just as much as their citizens, so they don't have a lot of extra money to help those who are living on the street. They cannot afford to provide shelter and assistance to the growing number of homeless citizens. And when city and state budgets are stretched to the brink, too, the homeless population often falls through the cracks.

But all cities aren't coping with homelessness in the same way. While some metropolitan areas deal with it by passing new laws and arresting homeless people, others seek alternative methods to address the problem.

The city of Cleveland, Ohio, has partnered with the Northeast Ohio Coalition for the Homeless. They have worked to bring individuals and groups that serve food to the homeless together to talk about how to improve services. This allows agencies to coordinate their outreach efforts so that they avoid duplicating food provisions and, in turn, create a more orderly food-sharing system. The partnership is also working to provide an indoor food-sharing site for groups that wish to use it.

Portland, Oregon, has enacted a ten-year plan that includes the "A Key Not a Card" program. Outreach workers from five different organizations are able to immediately offer people living on the street permanent housing, rather than just a business card—thus, a key, not a card. During the first four years, from 2005 to 2009, 963 individuals in 451 households have been housed through the program. That number includes 216 that were placed directly from the street.

In Seattle, Washington, the 1811 Eastlake project provides supportive housing for seventy-five formerly homeless men and women living with chronic alcohol addiction. Project leaders work with county officials to identify those who are the most frequent users of crisis services. The residents receive twenty-four-hour, seven-day-a-week support services. These services include on-site mental health and chemical dependency treatment, heath care, daily meals, and community-building activities, among others. The first-year analysis of the 1811 Eastlake project found that it saved the county $2.5 million in one year by significantly reducing participants' medical expenses, county jail bookings, sobering center usage, and shelter usage. The savings more than covered the program's $1.1 million operating cost.

Another city seeking alternative methods to handle its homelessness problem is Daytona Beach, Florida. To help reduce panhandling on city streets, a coalition of service providers, business groups, and the City of Daytona Beach began a program that provides homeless participants with jobs and housing. Called the "Downtown Street Team," the program's participants are hired to clean up downtown and are initially provided with shelter and then with transitional housing. Many participants in the program move on to full-time jobs and permanent housing.

Other cities have addressed their homelessness problem in a different way. In Nashville, Tennessee, a tent village housing homeless people sprang up beneath an overpass on public land near the Cumberland River. At first, the city posted eviction notices in the camp. But after a few months, the mayor of Nashville suspended those notices and opted for a different approach to the problem. Knowing the city's homeless shelters were at capacity and unable to admit any new people, the government decided to allow the tent city to remain standing. With the help of several local nonprofits, Nashville is now servicing the tent city, providing portable toilets, trash pickup, a mobile medical van, and visits from social workers. Volunteers bring firewood to the camp's residents during the colder winter months.

Similar tent camps have popped up in other cities across the United States. In Lacey, Washington, a church started a homeless camp in its parking lot after the city changed local ordinances to permit it. And in Ventura, California, the city council revised its laws to permit sleeping in cars overnight in some areas.

Regardless of how cities respond, it is clear that the recession has worsened the homelessness problem. Many cities don't know how to respond to the rapidly expanding homeless population. They often don't have the extra money to build shelters and provide housing. And while cities are trying to cope as best they can, there likely won't be any real relief to the problem until the recession ends.

Because of the recession, many people have lost jobs, which in turn, causes them to lose their homes. They are forced to find other forms of shelter, such as tents.

5 Ending Homelessness

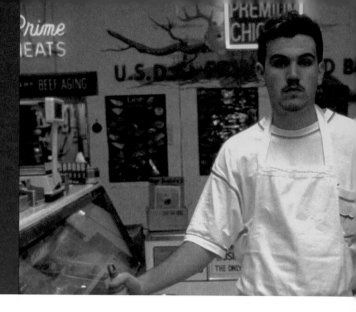

One of the key ways to fight homelessness is through public policy and legislation. By changing laws and enacting economic policies that benefit the poor, the U.S. homelessness rate could drop significantly.

As the nation struggles economically, the government has acted to help the poor by raising the minimum wage. By raising the minimum wage, which is the least amount that a worker can earn as determined by law, the government helps the poor in several ways. First, it immediately impacts those working minimum-wage jobs. They instantly get a raise, which will help them pay their bills and rent. It also affects those who are a little higher on the pay scale, as their pay will need to be adjusted because those working below them will now make more money.

Another way that politicians can help alleviate the problem of homelessness is to create and subsidize more affordable housing. Working through federal agencies like HUD, government officials can enact policies that will help the homeless. Setting aside funds to build more affordable housing developments and homes—as well as offering vouchers and other financial aid—are ways the government can help the homeless and those on the verge of homelessness.

In addition to ensuring adequate income and housing, government leaders can assist the homeless and those on the verge of homelessness by making social services easily accessible. Social services such as health care, childcare, mental health care, and substance abuse treatment are essential for those trying to avoid homelessness. When these services are available and affordable, people can get the help that they need to stay healthy and off the streets.

There are other legislative measures that are geared toward helping the homeless. The Homeless Children and Youth Act, which has been promoted by the National Policy and Advocacy Council on Homelessness, amends the HUD definition of homeless to include children, youth, and their families. It also streamlines the process of referral by schools and community programs of children at risk of homelessness. Finally, it gives the community more power to serve homeless citizens, rather than having to rely solely on government assistance.

People working minimum-wage jobs often struggle to afford housing and bills. Without affordable housing options, they're at risk for homelessness.

When political leaders create laws and policy to benefit the homeless population, they make great strides toward ending the problem of homelessness altogether.

The Health Care Safety Net Act of 2008 designated money to the building and upkeep of health centers for impoverished Americans. The act also mandates studies concerning school-based health care centers and their impact on students' health and the U.S. Department of Health and Human Services' efforts to expand and improve care at health centers, among other things.

Advocacy Groups

There are many groups in the United States that are dedicated to ending homelessness and helping those currently suffering from it. These groups work on both a legislative and a personal level to achieve these goals. They lobby the U.S. Congress to pass legislation that will benefit those who suffer from homelessness or who are at risk of becoming homeless. And they work directly with those they are fighting for, providing assistance financially, mentally, and socially.

One of the major groups working to fight homelessness is the National Coalition for the Homeless. The nonprofit is a nationwide network of people who currently are or have experienced homelessness, activists and advocates, community-based and faith-based service providers, and volunteers. The coalition began in

The National Policy and Advocacy Council on Homelessness (NPACH) is one of many nonprofit groups that works to help end homelessness through government policy changes.

New York City in the early 1980s, when founder Robert Hayes filed a lawsuit on behalf of a homeless man in the city. The lawsuit was settled out of court, and as a result, homeless people in New York City were given the right to shelter.

The coalition engages in public education, policy advocacy, and grassroots organizing. Its focus is on four areas: housing justice, health care justice, economic justice, and civil rights. One of its major projects is the Bring America Home Act, a legislative proposal for the federal government to address the causes and consequences of homelessness. The coalition also works to register homeless people to vote, protect the civil rights of homeless people, and bring general awareness to the plight of the homeless.

Another group working to help the homeless is the National Center on Family Homelessness. It was started in the 1980s by David Jordan, former editor in chief of *Better Homes and Gardens*, and Dr. Ellen L. Bassuk, a Harvard University professor. The organization primarily focuses on homeless families and children. It conducts research, identifies the best practices and solutions for dealing with homelessness, and works to raise public awareness of homeless families. The studies conducted on family homelessness are used to help local and national leaders develop effective policy to end homelessness.

The National Health Care for the Homeless Council (NHCHC) is made up of agencies, individuals, clinicians, advocates, and even homeless people. The organization works to advance the cause of human rights and access to health care for poor and homeless Americans.

The NHCHC carries out this mission in a number of ways. It advocates for universal health care and for improvements to the current systems intended to serve the poor and homeless. It researches critical health care issues and publishes newsletters and other publications on the subject of health care for those suffering from poverty. Finally, it trains and organizes heath care providers, service agencies, and homeless people to help improve care.

The mission of the National Law Center on Homelessness and Poverty is to prevent and end home-lessness by serving as the legal arm of the movement to end homelessness. It accomplishes this by working in impact litigation, policy advocacy, and public education. It represents the needs of homeless people in the courts, working to fight the causes of poverty and discrimina-tion against them.

The National Center for Children in Poverty works to help children suffering from poverty and homelessness. The group was founded in 1989 as a public policy center dedicated to promoting economic security, health, and well-being for America's low-income families and children.

It conducts research studies to help lawmakers create public policy that will help the poor.

The Youth, Homelessness, and Education project is one of the National Center for Children in Poverty's big projects. It focuses on youth ages twelve to seventeen who are homeless or who have experienced homelessness. It examines data on these youth to determine the effects of homelessness on the likelihood of a child graduating from high school or being educationally successful.

Also focusing on the education of homeless youth is the National Association for the Education of Homeless Children and Youth. This grassroots group formed in 1989 to ensure that children and youth residing in temporary living situations receive equal services through public schools across the country. Working with parents, educators, advocates, and researchers, it monitors school enrollment and attendance for homeless children. By doing this, the group helps make certain that homeless children regularly attend school so that they'll have the same opportunity for educational success as children with permanent homes.

The National Association of Education of Homeless Children and Youth administers the LeTendre Education Fund. This scholarship program provides academic funding, resources, and mentoring to students who are homeless or who have experienced homelessness.

The National Alliance to End Homelessness is a nonprofit group that works to prevent and end homelessness. It acts to influence public policy to benefit homeless people and those at risk of homelessness. In addition, it gets involved on the community level, working with local groups to promote education and research.

Assisting the homeless population on a federal level, HUD works to provide affordable housing for low-income families. Its mission is to increase home ownership, support community development, and increase access to affordable housing free from discrimination. It works with community-based and faith-based organizations to reach out to the neediest people within communities. HUD builds housing developments and individual homes that are available for low-income families to buy. These homes provide housing to many families who wouldn't be able to afford housing otherwise.

Another group that helps build homes for homeless and low-income families is Habitat for Humanity. This organization was founded in 1976 by Millard and Linda Fuller as a way for low-income families to help build affordable permanent housing for themselves. Relying on donations and volunteer labor, Habitat for Humanity builds and renovates homes for people who couldn't afford a house otherwise. The future homeowners work right along with the volunteers, laboring to help build their own homes. In the years since the organization was founded, it has built hundreds of thousands of homes around the world, providing permanent shelter for millions of people. There are also local partnerships and coalitions being forged between schools, police departments, social services agencies, and others that focus specifically on supporting homeless youth and families.

How You Can Help

Learning the facts about homelessness—and the sad reality of the situation for those living it—can make many people want to do something to help. Many think there is nothing that they can do to help. But the truth is, there is much that regular people—including children and teens—can do to help those who are less fortunate than themselves.

- Volunteer. Volunteering time to work directly with people experiencing homelessness is one of the best ways to learn about the situation and do something to help. There are many ways to volunteer time, whether it is sorting clothes at a donation center, serving meals at a soup kitchen, or helping with office duties at a shelter. A good place to find volunteer opportunities is the local United Way office.

Habitat for Humanity volunteers work to build affordable housing for the poor. Volunteers of all ages are encouraged to help Habitat in its work to help those living in poverty.

- Help build homes. Habitat for Humanity is always in need of volunteers of all ages. The organization has a youth program that offers volunteer opportunities to children and youth. Children ages five to eight can pitch in by being helpers to other volunteers and by participating in a number of other child-friendly activities affiliated with the organization. Kids ages nine to thirteen can contribute by being planners, fund-raisers, and press agents for the organization. Youth ages fourteen to twenty-five can participate in campus chapters of Habitat for Humanity, and those sixteen and up can actually help build houses.

- Donate clothing/toys. Most people have clothing they've outgrown or no longer want, as well as toys, games, and other items. Those things might be unwanted by one person, but for a homeless person, they could be a wonderful gift. Whether it's that coat or pair of shoes that have been outgrown, or toys that have long been set aside, shelters and other organizations that assist the homeless can always use gently used clothing and toys.

- Educate others. Many people know very little about homeless people. They think of homeless people as stereotypes, rather than thinking of them as simply people. Spreading the word to those who are less informed helps break down some of the negative stereotypes about homeless people. It also helps open others' eyes to the problem of homelessness, and it creates a stronger sense of compassion toward those who are without homes.

- Change your behavior. Removing words like "bum," "beggar," and "hobo" from your vocabulary when referencing homeless people is a tiny way to make a huge difference. These words are hurtful to those experiencing homelessness, and removing them from your vocabulary will encourage those around you to do the same. Another way to adjust behavior to help the homeless population is by simply smiling or speaking to them as you would any other person. Treating them like the human beings they are helps make their situation a little less difficult.

More and more people are likely to become homeless before the nation gets back on its feet financially. That doesn't mean they are bad people or are any less important or likable than people with permanent homes. It just means they have gotten into a bad situation financially and need some help to get back on track. As the United States works to recover from this recession, everyone must remember that the economy has affected many people. In some cases, it has affected people we know and interact with on a regular basis. And by being more aware of homelessness and learning the truth about it and refusing to listen to or repeat stereotypes, people are doing a small thing that will go a long way to solving this problem for good.

Glossary

advocate To work on behalf of those who cannot defend or help themselves; someone who works on behalf of others.

bankruptcy A legal declaration that a person is unable to repay his or her debts. In most cases, the debts are wiped clean and the person gets a bad credit rating.

communicable disease A disease that can easily be transmitted from one person to another through sneezing, coughing, etc.

default The act of failing to meet a financial obligation, such as failing to pay back a loan.

depression A long-term economic state characterized by unemployment, reduced spending, low levels of trade and investment, and a decline in the GDP of more than 10 percent.

economy A monetary system of production, distribution, and consumption of products.

foreclosure A situation in which a homeowner is unable to make principal and/or interest payments on his or her mortgage. As a result, the lender can seize and sell the property according to the terms of the mortgage contract.

gross domestic product (GDP) The GDP is a basic measure of a country's economic performance based on the market value of goods produced within that country. In other words, a country's GDP is a measurement of the value of its exported products, such as food, cars, etc.

homelessness The state of lacking a fixed, regular, and adequate nighttime residence.

layoff The loss of a job due to a company reducing the number of its employees, usually because of lowered company profits. Layoffs differ from being fired because they usually are not based on employee wrongdoing.

minimum wage The lowest wage a business can legally pay an employee, according to federal standards.

mortgage The transfer of an interest in property to a lender as a security for a debt, usually a loan of money.

panhandle To beg or ask for money in a public place, usually on a street or sidewalk.

poverty The state of having little or no money and few or no material possessions.

recession A general slowdown of economic activity for a prolonged period of time, usually lasting six months to a year.

subsidy A grant paid by a government to an enterprise that benefits the public.

unemployment The state of having no job; joblessness.

voucher A certificate that can be used to pay for certain things, such as housing, health care, and education.

For More Information

Habitat for Humanity International
121 Habitat Street
Americus, GA 31709 USA
(800) 422-4828
Web site: http://www.habitat.org
Habitat for Humanity seeks to eliminate poverty housing
and homelessness from the world by building homes
for those in need.

Homelessness Partnering Strategy
Human Resources and Skills Development Canada
Service Canada
Ottawa, ON K1A 0J9
Canada
(800) 622-6232
Web site:
http://www.hrsdc.gc.ca/eng/homelessness/index.shtml
The Homelessness Partnering Strategy is a program that relies
on communities to determine their own needs and develop
appropriate projects to fight homelessness in Canada.

National Center on Family Homelessness
181 Wells Avenue
Newton, MA 02459

(617) 964-3834
Web site: http://www.familyhomelessness.org
The National Center on Family Homelessness raises public awareness about the unique needs of homeless families.

National Coalition for the Homeless
2201 P Street NW
Washington, DC 20037
(202) 462-4822
Web site: http://www.nationalhomeless.org
The National Coalition for the Homeless is a national network of people who are currently experiencing or who have experienced homelessness, activists and advocates, community-based and faith-based service providers, and others committed to ending homelessness.

National Law Center on Homelessness & Poverty
1411 K Street NW, Suite 1400
Washington, DC 20005
(202) 638-2535
Web site: http://www.nlchp.org
The mission of National Law Center on Homelessness & Poverty is to prevent and end homelessness by serving as the legal arm of the national movement to end homelessness.

Raising the Roof
200-263 Eglinton Avenue West
Toronto, ON M4R 1B1
Canada
(416) 481-1838
Web site: http://www.raisingtheroof.org
Raising the Roof works to end homelessness in Canada by funding local grassroots agencies, building awareness about homelessness, and building partnerships between groups that can help end homelessness.

Web Sites

Due to the changing nature of Internet links, Rosen Publishing has developed an online list of Web sites related to the subject of this book. This site is updated regularly. Please use this link to access the list:

http://www.rosenlinks.com/itn/home

For Further Reading

Berger Kaye, Cathryn. *A Kids' Guide to Hunger and Homelessness: How to Take Action!* Minneapolis, MN: Free Spirit Publishing, 2007.

Blank, Jessica. *Almost Home*. New York, NY: Hyperion Books, 2007.

Cooley, Beth. *Shelter*. New York, NY: Delacorte Books for Young Readers, 2006.

Gunning, Monica. *A Shelter in Our Car*. San Francisco, CA: Children's Book Press, 2004.

Hopper, Kim. *Reckoning with Homelessness* (Anthropology of Contemporary Issues). Ithaca, NY: Cornell University Press, 2003.

Hubbard, Jim. *Lives Turned Upside Down: Homeless Children in Their Own Words and Photographs*. New York, NY: Aladdin, 2007.

Knoop, Todd Alan. *Recessions and Depressions: Understanding Business Cycles*. Santa Barbara, CA: Praeger, 2004.

Morrell, Jessica P. *Voices from the Street: Truths About Homelessness from Sisters of the Road*. Vancouver, WA: Gray Sunshine, 2007.

Nagle, Jeanne. *How a Recession Works* (Real World Economics). New York, NY: Rosen Publishing Group, 2009.

Bibliography

Bureau of Labor Statistics. "Labor Force Statistics from the Current Population Survey." U.S. Department of Labor. Retrieved September 10, 2009 (http://www.bls.gov/cps).

City Mayors Society. "Hunger and Homelessness Increase in American Cities." CityMayors.com, December 14, 2008. Retrieved August 29, 2009 (http://www.citymayors.com/features/uscity_poverty.html).

Economist. "Diagnosing Depression." December 20, 2008. Retrieved September 10, 2009 (http://www.economist.com/businessfinance/display Story.cfm?story_id=12852043).

Habitat for Humanity "Fact Sheet." Retrieved August 7, 2009 (http://www.habitat.org/how/factsheet.aspx).

Hopper, Kim. *Reckoning with Homelessness* (Anthropology of Contemporary Issues). Ithaca, NY: Cornell University Press, 2003.

Knoop, Todd Alan. *Recessions and Depressions: Understanding Business Cycles.* Santa Barbara, CA: Praeger, 2004.

Labonte, Mark, and Patrick Purcell. *Recession, Depression, Insolvency, Bankruptcy, and Federal Bailouts.* Alexandria, VA: TheCapitol.Net, Inc., 2009.

Levitz, Jennifer. "Cities Tolerate Homeless Camps." *Wall Street Journal*, August 11, 2009. Retrieved

September 10, 2009 (http://online.wsj.com/article/SB124994409537920819.html).

McKinley, Jesse. "Cities Deal with a Surge in Shantytowns." *New York Times*, March 26, 2009. Retrieved September 10, 2009 (http://www.nytimes.com/2009/03/26/us/26tents.html).

Morrell, Jessica P. *Voices from the Street: Truths About Homelessness from Sisters of the Road*. Vancouver, WA: Gray Sunshine, 2007.

National Alliance to End Homelessness. "Highest CoC Homeless Population and Rates." Retrieved August 9, 2009 (http://www.endhomelessness.org/section/data/interactivemaps/homelessratesbycoc).

National Association for the Education of Homeless Children and Youth. "Facts About the Education of Children and Youth Experiencing Homelessness." Retrieved August 8, 2009 (http://www.naehcy.org/facts.html).

National Center on Family Homelessness. "Children." Retrieved August 8, 2009 (http://www.familyhome-lessness.org/?q=node/5).

National Center on Family Homelessness. "Families." Retrieved August 8, 2009 (http://www.familyhome-lessness.org/?q=node/4).

National Coalition for the Homeless. "Homes, Not Handcuffs: The Criminalization of Homeless in U.S. Cities." Retrieved September 1, 2009 (http://www.nationalhomeless.org/publications/crim-report/index.html).

National Coalition for the Homeless. "How Many People Experience Homelessness?" Retrieved July 20, 2009 (http://www.nationalhomeless.org/factsheets/ How_Many.html).

National Law Center on Homelessness and Poverty. "Homelessness and Poverty in America: Real Solutions." Retrieved September 1, 2009 (http://www.nlchp.org/hapia_solutions.cfm).

National Policy and Advocacy Council on Homelessness. "Facts About H.R. 29, the Homeless Children and Youth Act of 2009." Retrieved September 15, 2009 (http://npach.org/HCYA).

Now. "Facts and Figures: The Homeless." PBS.org, June 26, 2009. Retrieved September 10, 2009 (http://www.pbs.org/now/shows/526/homeless-facts.html).

Oregon State Bar. "Understanding Bankruptcy." Retrieved July 30, 2009 (http://www.osbar.org/public/pamphlets/bankruptcy.html).

U.S. Courts. "Bankruptcy Statistics." Retrieved August 25, 2009 (http://www.uscourts.gov/bnkrpctystats/ bankruptcystats.htm).

Index

About the Author

Jennifer Bringle has spent a great deal of time getting to know homeless individuals through volunteer work at a local soup kitchen. While researching this book, she learned even more about the plight of those without homes. In addition to writing nonfiction books for young adults, she writes for several newspapers and magazines.

Photo Credits

Cover (top left) Shutterstock; cover (top right) © Joe McNally/Getty Images; cover (bottom), 28, 32 © Justin Sullivan/Getty Images; pp. 4, 6 © Paul J. Richards/AFP/Getty Images; p. 5 © www.istockphoto.com/Rich Legg; p. 10 © Bruce Ayres/Getty Images; pp. 12, 14 © Hulton Archive/Getty Images; p. 13 © Yellow Dog Productions/Getty Images; p. 17 © www.istockphoto.com/Lev Olkha; pp. 19, 22 © Rex Ziak/Getty Images; p. 20 © Nicole Bengiveno/The New York Times/Redux Pictures; p. 24 © Spencer Platt/Getty Images; p. 26 © Marilyn K. Yee/The New York Times/Redux Pictures; p. 29 © www.istockphoto.com/Vasiliki Varvaki; p. 30 © Bill Pugliano/Getty Images; pp. 35, 41, 51 © AP Images; p. 38 © Mike Simons/Getty Images; pp. 42, 44 © Michael L. Abramson/Time Life Pictures/Getty Images; p. 45 © The National Policy and Advocacy Council on Homelessness.

Designer: Tom Forget; Editor: Bethany Bryan;
Photo Researcher: Marty Levick